EXTREME ENVIRONMENTAL THREATS™

DISAPPEARING FORESTS

Deforestation, Desertification, and Drought

Corona Brezina

ROSEN PUBLISHING®

New York

Published in 2009 by The Rosen Publishing Group, Inc.
29 East 21st Street, New York, NY 10010

Library of Congress Cataloging-in-Publication Data

Brezina, Corona.
Disappearing forests : deforestation, desertification, and drought / Corona Brezina.
    p. cm.—(Extreme environmental threats)
ISBN-13: 978-1-4358-5018-7 (library binding)
ISBN-13: 978-1-4358-5374-4 (pbk)
ISBN-13: 978-1-4358-5378-2 (6 pack)
1. Deforestation—Juvenile literature. 2. Desertification—Juvenile literature. 3. Droughts—Juvenile literature. I. Title.
SD418.B74 2009
333.75—dc22

                                                                            2008018812

Manufactured in the United States of America

CPSIA Compliance Information: Batch #BR015250YA: For Further Information Contact Rosen Publishing, New York, New York at 1-800-237-9932

On the cover: Horses graze over newly burned rain forest in Brazil. Brazilian farmers and ranchers routinely burn rain forest to graze cattle or to plant crops. **Title page:** Hundreds of acres of forest were sacrificed to supply this load of cut timber.

Contents

	INTRODUCTION	4
1	THE FOREST PRIMEVAL	7
2	A VALUABLE RESOURCE	18
3	HUMAN IMPACT ON FORESTS	30
4	THE FORESTS OF TOMORROW	43
	GLOSSARY	55
	FOR MORE INFORMATION	57
	FOR FURTHER READING	59
	BIBLIOGRAPHY	60
	INDEX	62

INTRODUCTION

This is rain forest in
Bolivia's Tuichi River valley.
A proposed dam would
flood the region and create
a lake of one thousand
square miles.

A lush canopy of greenery is suspended high above
the forest floor. Birds and small animals occupy the
high branches, while larger mammals browse on berries
or graze far below. Amphibians, reptiles, fish, and
insects all have their specialized niches in the forest.
Unseen, bacteria and fungi work to recycle dead
organic matter.

With some variation, this forest scene could take
place on any of the earth's six continents. Forests
across the world fulfill some essential functions, such as

providing habitat for life forms and protecting soil and water resources. Plant life plays a role in the carbon cycle, the process by which carbon moves through living organisms and the environment. Since elevated levels of carbon dioxide (CO_2) contribute to climate change, forests perform an important service by absorbing CO_2.

Although forests across the world share some characteristics, each forest has evolved into a unique ecosystem depending on factors such as climate, soil type, and moisture levels. Tropical rain forests take up a relatively small proportion of the earth's total area, but they host a spectacular range of biodiversity—20 percent of all species live in the Amazon rain forest alone. By contrast, the boreal forest of the far north, which spans vast tracts of land across Asia, Europe, and North America, supports a smaller variety of trees and wildlife.

Forests are a precious natural resource, but today they are under threat across the world. They are being logged, burned, cleared, and degraded. Most often, deforestation results from land being converted for agricultural purposes, although forests are also decimated for timber and wood used for fuel.

When managed capably, forests can flourish as havens for natural life while also providing human communities with wood, employment, and ecological services. It remains to be seen, however, whether the human race will be able to meet the challenge of forest conservation and sustainable development that is crucial to the survival of these endangered and essential cradles of life.

THE FOREST PRIMEVAL

Scientists learn about the evolutionary development of plants from fossil records, such as the petrified forests, shown here, in Yellowstone National Park.

The first trees and forests emerged during the Devonian period, which lasted from 417 to 355 million years ago. Before this time, plants had no true roots or leaves. There was no soil yet, since soil consists of decomposing organic matter and microorganisms, as well as inorganic rock particles and minerals. The small, simple plants that did exist reproduced through spores. Moss forests and mats of bacteria and algae represented the bulk of the vegetation, along with some primitive rooted plants that began to generate soil.

This artist's conception of a Devonian landscape depicts extinct plant life from 408 to 374 million years ago, including palm-like trees and several species of groundcover.

THE EMERGENCE OF PLANTS, TREES, AND GRASSES

During the late Devonian period, there was a sudden surge in the development of plant life. Forests of fern-like trees with woody trunks spread across the land. Competition for resources, such as light or moisture, led to the development of diverse species adapted to different niches in the ecosystem. By the end of the Devonian period, the first seed-bearing plants had appeared. Microorganisms, vertebrates, and arthropods evolved alongside this proliferation of plant life.

Most of the coal that we use for fuel today dates from the Carboniferous period (354 to 291 million years ago). Coal is the fossilized remains of organic matter that once thrived in tropical forested swamps. The first conifers—cone-bearing trees such as pines—emerged during the Carboniferous period. The ginkgo tree, sometimes referred to as a "living fossil" since it still exists today, appeared during the Permian period (290 to 249 million years ago). Flowering plants, known by the scientific term "angiosperms," did not evolve until the late Jurassic period (205 to 143 million years ago).

The Cenozoic era, which extends from 65 million years ago to the present day, saw the emergence of another crucial form of plant life: grasses. During the late Cenozoic era, grasslands became widespread in some regions of the world, such as parts of North America. The forests retreated into smaller patches of woodland. Grasses were better able to withstand wildfire or grazing than were trees and plants, since the roots could send up new growth if the leaves were damaged. The bountiful grasslands also supported the evolution of grazing animals such as horses and various deerlike mammals, many of which are now extinct.

The evolution of plant life reflects constant and ongoing adaptation to changes in the earth's environment.

Factors such as temperatures, moisture levels, and atmospheric composition have all varied greatly over the ages. At times, the earth's poles have been free of ice, and much of the present-day United States would have been in a subtropical climate zone. Life forms have had to adjust in order to survive. In a process called speciation, a species gradually evolves into several different species adapted to specific new habitats. The opposite process is extinction. Some species survive but go into decline, edged out by others that are better suited to certain growing conditions. As the early swamps gave way to drier conditions, for example, conifers replaced the swamp-loving ferns in some areas. Later, grasses would come to thrive during a period of cooling, becoming the dominant form of plant life in many places.

MASS EXTINCTIONS

The progression and evolution of life on Earth has not been a smooth process, though. Throughout prehistoric times, there were at least five mass extinction events in which at least half of all species died out. The best known is the extinction that occurred 65 million years ago, which led to the dinosaurs dying off. It is now generally accepted that the cause was a massive asteroid that struck the earth off of the coast of modern-day Mexico, triggering devastating consequences in the climate and

A theropod, a dinosaur that went extinct 65 million years ago, is part of the "Evolving Planet" exhibit (shown here) at Chicago's Field Museum of Natural History.

environment. The most catastrophic extinction event, however, occurred about 251 million years ago, at the end of the Permian period. Over 90 percent of all marine species became extinct, as did many other life forms, including about 70 percent of vertebrate species.

The causes and progression of mass extinction events are not fully understood. It is possible that there have been earlier asteroid impacts that affected life on Earth. Geological events could have caused extreme environmental changes. Early shifting of the continents could have resulted in a turnover in life forms. Episodes of violent volcanic activity could have spewed greenhouse gases such as carbon dioxide and sulfur dioxide into the atmosphere, leading to periods of global warming or cooling. Similarly, there could have been a release of methane—another greenhouse gas—from the sea floor. Any of these circumstances could trigger a cascading series of events that could affect climate, temperature, sea levels, and the composition of the earth's atmosphere.

Plants are less vulnerable to mass extinction events than are animal life forms. Roots can sometimes survive underground and eventually grow back. Seeds can reestablish plant life after individual specimens are destroyed. Nevertheless, a region's plant life tends to undergo radical rearrangements in the immediate aftermath of a mass extinction. Some species migrate into new areas and establish themselves as dominant, while others go into abrupt decline.

This fossilized palm frond came from a tree that grew in Wyoming over 50 million years ago during a period of subtropical climate.

For scientists studying the impact of present-day climate change, it is crucial to understand plants' evolution and adaptation to natural changes in the environment over the ages. Human activity is raising the amount of CO_2 in the atmosphere, which is causing an increase in the earth's temperature. The earth experienced a comparable rapid warming episode about 55 million years ago, when the temperature rose by about 10 degrees Fahrenheit (5.6 degrees Celsius) over a period of ten thousand years. The world's forests reacted quickly to the change. Subtropical plants moved northward, replacing temperate forests made up of trees such as relatives of modern-day sycamore and walnuts. Plant fossils found in Wyoming were similar to species growing in Texas and Louisiana at the time.

EARLY HUMAN FOREST MANAGEMENT

During much of the earth's lifetime, the planet has period-ically cycled in and out of ice ages. The most recent occurrence began about seventy thousand years ago. Massive sheets of ice advanced from the polar ice cap, covering North America as far south as Wisconsin. The interior of the continent was transformed into a frigid, rocky desert. In Europe, conifers migrated southward to the Mediterranean region, replacing trees such as citrus that required warmer temperatures. The Amazon region of South America may have been deforested.

The ice began to retreat twelve thousand years ago. Plant life forms began to shift to their present-day ranges. For the past eighty-five hundred years, the earth's climate has experienced a relatively warm and stable period.

During this time, humans began to multiply throughout every habitable zone of the earth. About

Easter Island

When Dutch explorer Jacob Roggeveen became the first European to land on remote Easter Island in 1722, he was startled to discover a thriving civilization. Scientists today believe the island was first settled around 1200 by the Rapanui, who settled there from other South Pacific islands. Their population probably grew slowly at first before eventually exploding as they learned to exploit the island's plants and animals. Eventually, they were organized and sophisticated enough to carve and erect massive stone statues—called moai—around the island's perimeter.

Roggeveen didn't realize it, but he was encountering a culture in decline. Later visitors reported that the Rapanui population had been decimated by famine and battles over the island's scarce resources. Researchers today believe that the islanders doomed themselves even before Roggeveen landed by cutting down the island's vast palm forests in order to build and move the moai. Without the forests, the island's topsoil eroded and many of the island's plant and bird species became extinct.

seven thousand years ago, with the advent of agriculture, people began transforming open spaces into cropland. About five thousand years ago, people began crafting tools out of metal. Ever since, there has been an accelerating trend of clearing forestlands and the constant development of tools and technology that could perform deforestation much more efficiently.

Even when the human population was made up of small groups of hunters and gatherers, they employed a basic but powerful weapon against forests and other vegetation: fire. Fire could be used to drive game toward hunting grounds. Burning also opened up dense, nearly impenetrable woodland, making it easier to hunt and travel. In the aftermath of a fire, many of the first plants to grow back provided desirable foods such as tubers, nuts, berries, and seeds. The use of fire could be carefully managed, as it was by some Native American tribes before the arrival of Europeans. Grassy fields immediately encircling a settlement were burned annually. The surrounding area, used for gathering food and hunting small game, was burned every few years. At the outskirts of a settlement, fire was used to thin underbrush from the forest every couple of decades or so. In some areas, regular burning created prairie land for buffalo and other grazers.

Early societies also utilized wood as a raw material. Wood provided housing materials and heat, as well as tools, weapons, and everyday items such as bowls and wheels. Artisans understood that certain types of wood were particularly well suited for specific purposes, such as crafting bows out of yew wood.

Gradually, humans began to shift to an agricultural lifestyle, clearing land for settlements, permanent cropland, and pasture. The plow and the axe were both developed around 4000 BCE. Humans still turned to the surrounding forest for fuel, timber, game, and

A painting from 1832 shows fire advancing on the North American prairie. Native Americans used fire to manage their lands.

food, and as settlements grew, their use of the forest's resources also increased. There is no doubt that early humans dramatically impacted the forest around them, but there is little prehistoric record remaining of the precise extent of this transformation.

THE DAWN OF MODERN DEFORESTATION

After the establishment of the Greek city-states, science and the arts flourished, and scholars left some of the first written records that give clues about the state of forests in ancient Greece. In a 313 BCE work called *The Enquiry into Plants*, a scholar named Theophrastus made the first systematic effort to describe and classify trees. Other writers referenced forests and trees in literature, poetry, and works on subjects such as agriculture and geography.

As the Greek city-states expanded and thrived, vast tracts of land were cleared for the cropland needed to feed the growing population. Livestock such as sheep and pigs were free to range on cropland and in forests, where their activities damaged the forest floor and stunted new growth. Trees were felled for fuel, and timber was used to construct buildings and the fleets of ships necessary for an economy that relied on trade by sea. Furnaces fueled by wood were used to manufacture bricks and smelt metal. As the land surrounding major cities such as Athens became deforested, timber and fuel wood had to be transported from longer and longer distances.

In a way, the exploitation and clearing of forests in ancient Greece represents a precursor to the modern treatment of forested land. Vast tracts of forest are still being cleared for agriculture, often by burning. Many forests are being degraded by logging and removal of other resources. As in ancient Greece, timber and other wood products are being transported from great distances. But today, humans have the means to transport wood easily from one continent to another. Present-day society is faced with the same issue of allocating the earth's limited resources among a growing population. In ancient Greece, logging and clearing land led to regional degradation of forested land. Today, however, unrestrained plundering of the world's forests could have global rather than merely local consequences.

This aerial view shows smoke billowing up from fires in the Ituri Forest in the Republic of Congo.

A forest is much more than just a collection of trees. A forest is a habitat that sustains biological diversity, providing a home for countless plants, animals, insects, microorganisms, and other life forms. Forests play a role in ecological processes such as the carbon cycle and the water cycle. The presence of a forest can influence the climate in nearby areas, and forested land as a whole helps keep the global climate stable. These qualities make forests a crucial component in the earth's ecological functioning. Throughout history, however, humans have viewed forests primarily as a valuable resource to be exploited. Only in modern times have people begun to appreciate the importance of practicing sustainable development—meeting human needs without depleting forests and otherwise degrading the environment.

A VITAL BIOME

Forests are one of the world's major biomes—regions that share ecological characteristics such as climate and plant life. A forest is loosely defined as land where at least 25 percent of the area is occupied by tree crowns. Each forest is unique, but forests across the world fulfill some common ecological services, whether they are tropical mangrove swamps or northern coniferous forests.

Plant life plays an important role in the carbon cycle. Through a process called photosynthesis, plants capture energy from sunlight and use it to convert CO_2 and water into carbohydrates—the organic matter that makes up plant tissue. Photosynthesis also produces oxygen as a byproduct, which animals use during respiration. When dead plant life decays, some of the carbon in the tissue is stored and some is cycled back into the atmosphere.

Photosynthesis and respiration are only two of the processes in the carbon cycle. The entire cycle also involves carbon circulated through the oceans and stored in reservoirs such as limestone and fossil fuels. When humans burn fossil fuels such as coal and oil, this stored carbon is released into the atmosphere as CO_2. The natural processes that cycle CO_2 out of the atmosphere—such as photosynthesis—cannot handle the excess CO_2 being released by human activity. Therefore, levels of CO_2 in the atmosphere have been steadily increasing ever since the Industrial Revolution. Elevated levels of atmospheric CO_2 are responsible for climate change.

Forests are vital to the carbon cycle. By reducing the world's forests while at the same time releasing more and more carbon emissions, humans are unbalancing the cycle. In addition, clearing forests actually releases more atmospheric CO_2. When the trees and other plant matter decompose or are burnt, some of the carbon stored in their tissues returns to the atmosphere where it traps heat, resulting in even higher surface temperatures and climate change.

Forests also affect the water cycle, in which water evaporates from oceans and lakes, falls in the form of precipitation, and eventually seeps back to the oceans and lakes. Trees and other plants take part in the cycle through a process called transpiration. Roots absorb water from the ground. This water is then transported through the plant's trunk or stem. Eventually, it evaporates out of pores in the needles or leaves. This increases the atmospheric humidity, which influences the local climate. Clearing a forest can diminish humidity and rainfall in a region.

During heavy rains, forests reduce runoff by percolating water into the soil. This helps prevent flooding. The process also recharges groundwater reservoirs, which can alleviate potential dry spells in the future. Since humans also draw on underground water sources, forests provide a service by filtering water through the soil on the forest floor, thus purifying it.

Forests enrich the soil through the decomposition of organic matter. The forest canopy and undergrowth shield the soil from being baked dry by the sun, pummeled by precipitation, and buffeted by wind. Forests cycle nutrients into streams and provide shade. Tree roots hold the soil in place and prevent erosion, especially in hilly areas. Living organisms in the soil also help bind it together. When land is clear cut, fertile topsoil begins to wash away. This can sometimes lead to a process called mass wasting, in which rocks and soil cascade down hillsides, leaving behind barren wasteland.

Plant life in forests is organized into layers and niches. There is an upper canopy of tall trees and a second canopy of shorter species. Beneath these are shrubs and bushes that form the undergrowth, then the grasses, flowers, and other plant life that grow on the forest floor. Vines twine up tree trunks and along the ground.

This diagram shows a tree's water transport system, through which water is taken up by root hairs, transported through the plant's tissues, and lost through the leaves.

Forests provide food and habitat for a population of interconnected organisms. The life forms in an ecosystem are organized in a food web of producers (plants), consumers, and decomposers. Among consumers, herbivores feed on plants, carnivores feed on meat, and omnivores feed on a combination of plants and other life forms. Birds may eat both seeds and insects, for example. Decomposers such as fungi and bacteria break down dead material and waste.

Forests, especially tropical rain forests, are the most biologically diverse of the earth's biomes. About two-thirds of all plants and animals depend on forests for habitat. Forests contain a diversity of different ecosystems and species of organisms, as well as genetic diversity within species. Genetic diversity gives a species a greater ability to adapt to changes in environmental conditions.

TYPES OF FORESTS

There are many different criteria that can be used to classify the world's forests. When many people envision an idealized forest, they picture a primary, or old growth, forest—native forest that has been largely undisturbed by human activity. Only about 36 percent of the world's forests are primary forests, according to the FAO (the Food and Agriculture Organization of the United Nations). Most forests are managed with the intent to balance conservation with human use. If a forest undergoes a disturbance—whether a natural event such as a fire or human-caused disruption such as logging—it recovers through secondary succession, a sequence of stages of regrowth.

Forests are generally classified according to a combination of traits, such as climate, soil, geographic locale, and dominant species of trees. The most basic division is between temperate/boreal forests and tropical forests. Temperate and boreal forests occur in cooler regions, both on northern and southern continents. Tropical forests grow in warmer climates near the earth's equator.

The World Conservation Monitoring Center, part of the United Nations Environment Program, classifies forests into six broad categories. The first is temperate needleleaf, the world's most widespread type of forest. Mostly composed of coniferous trees, these forests grow in the northern latitudes and at high altitudes. They can withstand marginal soil, cold temperatures, and a short growing season.

Further south, the needleleaf forests give way to temperate broadleaf forests and mixed forests of coniferous and broadleaf trees. Most broadleaf trees—such as oak, maple, and sycamore—are deciduous, meaning that they lose their leaves every year. These forests range in temperate regions across the world, including the United States, Europe, China, Japan, Chile, Australia, and New Zealand.

Tropical moist forests consist of a wide variety of forest types, including lowland evergreen broadleaf rain forests. These are the tropical rain forests that are so rich in biodiversity that they contain over 40 percent of all plant and animal species within less than 3 percent of the world's land area. They are found mostly in the Amazon region of South America, the Congo Basin of Africa, and Indonesia and other Pacific islands. These rain forests receive over 80 inches (200 centimeters) of rain annually, and since they are located close to the equator, they experience little variation in seasons or length of day. The soil in the rain forest is generally infertile. Most of the nutrients are stored in the lush vegetation, and decomposers such as insects, fungi, and microbes quickly recycle dead material.

Different tiers of the rain forest, from the high canopy down to the shaded undergrowth, contain separate micro-climates that each host a separate ecosystem. Most animals, birds, and reptiles live in the canopy. Because the soil is so poor, land cleared of rain forest—often through "slash and burn" methods—cannot sustain crops for more than a few years. Other major types of tropical moist forests include tropical coniferous forests, mangrove swamps, and montane forests (forests on tropical mountains).

A waterfall cascades through a lush Costa Rican rain forest, shown here. Costa Rica protects forested areas with high biodiversity through ambitious conservation programs.

Tropical dry forests grow in regions that experience seasonal droughts. They are composed mainly of deciduous trees that shed their leaves annually in order to survive the dry spells. Most of the world's tropical dry forests have been lost or are severely threatened.

The FAO has two other categories: sparse trees and parkland—areas with limited tree cover—and forest plantations. Forest plantations are planted by humans for timber and other wood products. They do not host the biodiversity of naturally occurring forests, but they provide some of the ecological services, such as protecting the soil and storing carbon.

THE HUMAN FOOTPRINT

Throughout history, agricultural clearing has been the primary cause of deforestation. As human population has increased, pastures and cultivated crops have pushed back the edges of forested land. From 1700 to 1850, during the rise of the industrial age, Europe lost about 62 million acres (25 million hectares) of forestland (as cited by Michael Williams in *Deforesting the Earth*). North America lost about 110 million acres (45 million hectares) between 1700 and 1850, and 67 million acres (27 million hectares) between 1850 and 1920.

The extent of loss is even greater in Latin America. The region saw rapid population growth during the twentieth century, and technological advances such as chainsaws and improved methods of transportation helped the acceleration of deforestation. Latin America lost 62 million acres (25 million hectares) between 1700 and 1850, 130 million acres (51 million hectares)

Mangrove Swamps

Mangrove swamps are a type of tropical moist forest that grow in coastal areas throughout the world. They are most common in Asian countries such as Vietnam and Malaysia, but they can also be found in New Zealand, Australia, the Caribbean, and even Florida. The mangroves themselves are highly adaptable, with about seventy different species from two dozen families. They can range from small shrubs to 200-foot-tall (60 meters) trees. These unique trees have the ability to filter salt from seawater, allowing them to live in tidal areas. Mangrove swamps provide habitats for plant and animal species and serve as nurseries for marine species.

Along with providing shelter for marine life, their root systems help prevent erosion by catching soil and other debris that would otherwise wash into the ocean. They also create a protective barrier that shields the coastline. Following the devastating 2004 tsunami in the Indian Ocean, it was found that areas with mangrove swamps along the coast sustained far less damage. Nevertheless, mangrove swamps are among the most threatened forests in the world, increasingly being converted to shrimp farms or destroyed to make room for human development on prime coastal real estate.

between 1850 and 1920, 240 million acres (96 million hectares) between 1920 and 1950, and 300 million acres (122 million hectares) between 1950 and 1980. Africa, Asia, and Australia also saw trends toward deforestation.

When an area is deforested, it loses not only the ecological services provided by the forest, but also the biodiversity within the ecosystem. This biodiversity is vital to the earth's well-being, and it also holds vital interest to science. Indigenous cultures across the world use native plants in traditional medicine. Most of these plants have not been thoroughly studied for their medicinal value. Considering that many modern medicines were initially derived from plants, it is probable that plants in rain forests or other wild habitats hold potentially lifesaving remedies. Many plants with known medicinal value are endangered or threatened, however, and some could become extinct without humans ever knowing of their existence.

Human appreciation of forests goes deeper than the value of their timber, ecological services, and scientific interest. Some cultures once worshipped sacred groves or particular trees. Many mythologies involve a "tree of life" such as Ygdrasil, the ash tree that extends through the worlds of Norse mythology. Forests have served as an inspiration for writers and artists.

Today, many Americans camp, fish, hunt, and hike in national forestland. Still, there is ongoing debate about appropriate use of this land. Environmentalists advocate preserving certain areas as roadless wilderness, while the timber industry and other interests push to open them up for development. Another point of controversy is how to prevent recreational use from damaging

Tamiflu, the drug used to combat bird flu, is derived from chemicals in star anise, pictured here. Other plants could hold the secret to the next miracle drug.

forestland. Snowmobiles and all-terrain vehicles (ATVs), for example, can damage forest trails, and some people believe that they should be restricted or banned in some sites.

In this Indonesian province of Riau, timber from a pulp wood plantation is loaded for transportation. Much of the region's primary forest has been cleared for forest plantations.

Forests provide both ecological services and valuable raw materials. Does humankind have to choose, therefore, between environmental well-being and economic progress? Increasingly, both environmentalists and business interests are beginning to agree that conservation makes good economic sense. This has led to an increased interest in sustainable development—the practice of managing the use of renewable resources in order to avoid depleting them.

SUSTAINABLE FOREST MANAGEMENT

A sustainable forest management plan must balance ecological and economic considerations. It should allow for an adequate area of forest coverage that includes different types of forests. Managers should support biological diversity within the forests, including conservation of biodiversity "hot spots" that occur in a few places in the world. They should protect the forests' health against threats such as wildfire, pollution, and invasive species. Some primary forest should be preserved, and harvesting for logs and other forest products should allow for future growth. In calculating a forest's value, the ecological services to the surrounding area must also be considered.

The forest may also provide jobs, recreation, and tourism draws for the surrounding community. In drawing up policies on forest management, decision makers should consider a wide variety of factors that could affect the success of the management plan, such as public opinion, scientific findings, and infrastructure.

Today, sustainable forest management worldwide is a goal, not a reality. Before human deforestation, forests covered about 40 percent of the earth's land mass. Today, that amount has been diminished to about 30 percent, an area of slightly less than one trillion

Here, tourists explore the rain forest in Barron Gorge National Park in Australia. Money from ecotourism can serve as an incentive for conservation of pristine forests.

acres (4 billion hectares), as reported by the 2005 Forest Resource Assessment (FRA) released by the FAO. The FAO has been monitoring worldwide forest coverage since 1946. Most of the world's forest—about 84 percent—is publicly owned.

The 2005 FRA found that deforestation was occurring at a rate of about 32 million acres (13 million hectares) per year, although some of that loss was offset by expansion of forested land in other places. Between 1990 and 2005, the world lost about 3 percent of its total forest area, with most of the deforestation occurring in tropical climates. Every year, more than 260 million acres (104 million hectares) of forest were affected by threats such as wildfire, insects, disease, or climatic events. Quite simply, the planet is losing one of its most valuable resources—absolutely essential to continued human life on Earth—at an alarming rate.

AFRICA AND THE MIDDLE EAST

Africa contains about 1.57 billion acres (635 million hectares) of forest, about 16 percent of the world's total forest area. There are tropical rain forests in the Congo Basin of central Africa—the Democratic Republic of Congo has the sixth largest area of forest of any country in the world—as well as a wide range of other forest types across the continent. Between 1990 and 2005, Africa accounted for about 55 percent of the world's forest loss, an area of about one billion acres (four million hectares). This amounts to over 9 percent of its forests. In many areas, civil conflict led to further deforestation and rampant forest fires. There were particularly high rates of forest loss in Sudan, Angola, Tanzania, Zambia, Zimbabwe, Cameroon, the Democratic Republic of Congo, and Nigeria.

Seven of the world's biodiversity hot spots (those places that provide a habitat for many rare and endangered species) are located in Africa. On one of these hot spots, the Indian island nation of Madagascar, there are clusters of baobabs, a deciduous tree found in Africa and Australia. Six species of the tree are native to Madagascar. The baobab can grow to over 80 feet (24 meters) tall and attain a trunk diameter of 10 feet (3 m) or more. Although they are difficult to date, they can live for hundreds of years. One of the tree's most remarkable

In this photograph, baobab trees tower over grassy plains in Madagascar. Baobabs store water in their barrel-like trunks in order to survive dry seasons.

traits is its ability to support biodiversity. Madagascar and the surrounding islands are home to over eleven thousand plant species, as well as a rich variety of birds, reptiles, amphibians, and mammals, including more than thirty different lemur species. Dozens of different life forms can inhabit a single baobab tree, each in a different biological niche. Below the canopy, other animals eat the tree's fruit and graze on the leaves.

One of the driest regions on Earth, the Middle East has very little forest cover. Only Lebanon, Cyprus, and Turkey have forests on over 10 percent of their land area. Since forested land can be highly prized where it is very rare, there has been significant investment in forest plantations in some parts of the Middle

East. In Kuwait, Oman, and the United Arab Emirates, the entire forested area consists of forest plantations.

ASIA, THE PACIFIC, AND AUSTRALIA

About one-third of the land area in Asia and the Pacific—including Australia—is forested, amounting to about 19 percent of the world's forests, a total of 1.81 billion acres (734 million hectares). The overall amount of forestland increased by 1.56 million acres (633,000 hectares) from 2000 to 2005. Forestation trends vary greatly from one area to another, however.

The overall increase was mainly due to reforestation efforts in China, mostly through planting of forest plantations. China has the world's fifth largest forest area—about 490 million acres (197 million hectares)—which includes about 175 million acres (71 million hectares) of planted forest. Bhutan, India, and Vietnam have also increased their forest area. Other parts of Asia and the Pacific islands experienced some of the most extreme deforestation anywhere in the world. Indonesia, Myanmar, Cambodia, the Philippines, and North Korea all lost forest area.

The case of Indonesia, whose forests are second only to Brazil in terms of biodiversity, is particularly tragic. A nation made up of 17,508 islands, Indonesia is the fourth most populous country in the world. Indonesia also has the eighth greatest forest area—217 million acres (88 million hectares)—of any country in the world. The biological diversity is so abundant that previously unknown species of plants and animals are frequently discovered in Indonesia's forests.

High levels of poverty and political unrest have contributed to large-scale deforestation and destruction of natural resources, however. Between 2000 and 2005, Indonesia lost an average of 4.7 million acres (1.9 million hectares) of forest every year. During this time, it saw a decrease of 13 percent of its primary forest area. The government has been unable to control illegal logging that has caused much of the forest loss.

EUROPE AND RUSSIA

Throughout the period from 1990 to 2005, forestland in Europe increased by 7 percent to a total area of 477 million acres (193 million hectares). Nearly half of this increase was due to the establishment of forest plantations. Europe has also seen an increase in a different category of planted forest—managed "seminatural" forests planted with species native to a region. The remaining increase resulted from agricultural land reverting to forest. Spain, Italy, Bulgaria, France, Portugal, and Greece saw the greatest gains in forest area. Due to extensive deforestation in past centuries, only 4 percent of Europe's forest consists of primary forest, far less than the worldwide average of 27 percent.

Europe and Russia are generally grouped together in discussions of forest due to geographical proximity and similarity of climate. With about 20 percent of the world's total forests—about 2 billion acres (809 million hectares)—Russia has the largest forest area of any country in the world. In Russia's southern latitudes, there are temperate mixed and broadleaf forests. The bulk of Russia's forested land is made up of boreal forest called the taiga. Half of the world's boreal forest falls within Russia's borders. One-third belongs to Canada, and the rest is found in Alaska and Scandinavia. Boreal forests do not have the biodiversity of tropical forests, with fewer than ten species of trees, mostly coniferous, dominating the vast expanses. Nevertheless, boreal forests make up a third of the world's forested area, and they play an important part in regulating climate and providing habitat for wildlife.

LATIN AMERICA AND THE CARIBBEAN

Along with Africa, Latin America and the Caribbean experienced the world's highest rates of deforestation between 1990 and 2005. The trend toward forest loss accelerated during this period—an average annual loss of .46 percent of all forest area during the 1990s rose to

.51 percent between 2000 and 2005. This amounts to the deforestation of a total area of 160 million acres (64 million hectares) for the fifteen-year period. There were areas of forest increase within the region, however. The Caribbean increased its overall forested area, largely through expanding forest plantations. Costa Rica experienced forest loss between 1990 and 2000, but added forest area from 2000 to 2005. Chile, Cuba, and Uruguay also increased in forest area.

Latin America and the Caribbean have some of the most abundant biodiversity of any region of the world, but they also have the highest number of threatened and endangered species. The region's forests are under assault. Loggers illegally harvest the endangered mahogany tree for its beautiful wood, leaving behind a devastated habitat. Forests are stripped of wood burned for fuel, and land is cleared for agriculture. Wildfires burn millions of hectares of forest annually. They were especially damaging in 1999, when 33.6 million acres (13.6 million hectares) were burned.

The largest amount of forest was lost in South America. South America's Amazon Basin, sometimes called Amazonia, supports the rain forest that is home to the world's richest concentration of biodiversity. The Amazon rain forest is 2 trillion acres (823 million hectares) in area and extends across nine different countries. Slightly over half of the Amazon rain forest is

As seen here, the Synya River runs through the winter landscape of Russia's Yugyd-Va National Park, part of the largest tract of primary boreal forest surviving in Europe.

located in Brazil. There is such variety of life in the Amazon that about 20 percent of the earth's species live there—millions of insect species, about fifty thousand plant species, thousands of bird and fish species, and hundreds of mammals, amphibians, and reptiles. The Amazon forest also plays an important role in climate control by cycling and storing carbon.

Although deforestation in Brazil slowed during 2005 and 2006, satellite images showed a sharp increase during the second half of 2007. The government began

This area of newly deforested land in Brazil was cleared for soybean cultivation. Since the land is not highly fertile, farmers will soon have to clear more rain forest for future crops.

an aggressive crackdown on illegal logging, but there is no easy solution for root causes of deforestation, such as poverty, that force people to squander the forest's resources. Environmentalists worry about the potentially devastating consequences if deforestation is not slowed. If too much forest area is lost, it could disrupt the water cycle and cause the ecosystem of the Amazon forest to become destabilized.

NORTH AMERICA

Canada, the United States, and Mexico all have considerable forest resources. North America accounts for 17 percent of the world's forests, a total of 1.67 billion acres (677 million hectares). Overall, North America saw almost no change in area between 1990 and 2005. The United States gained a small amount of forest area. Mexico lost some forests but at a much lower rate of deforestation than Central America. Canada reported no change.

One major shift in the United States's use of forest products concerns trade. The United States exports a significant amount of timber and other wood, but now the country is actually a net importer of wood products. Americans have started buying far more wood products, such as furniture, from other countries. This trend is a change from the early 1990s, when the United States exported more forest products than it imported.

In Canada, 92 percent of all forests are owned by the government, as are 42 percent of American and 59 percent of Mexican forests. Mexican public forests are managed on a community level, however, which means that local residents benefit from capable forest management. The FAO describes this system as "one of the world's most advanced models of community forest management" in its State of the World's Forests 2007 report.

Overall, 85 percent of all North American forestland is designated for production, meaning that trees can be harvested, or multiple use, meaning that trees can be either harvested or protected. In the United States, environmental groups closely monitor forest policy. Activities such as logging and other development in national forests can become controversial if people come to believe that the practices will negatively impact forest health.

North America is home to some spectacularly beautiful forests. Temperate rain forests stretch along Canada's Pacific coast and the shoreline of Alaska's Tongass National Forest. In California's sequoia groves, the majestic trees can grow to heights of more than 200 feet (61 m). Mexico's mountainous Madrean Pine-Oak Woodlands, home to 25 percent of all of Mexico's species, is one of the earth's biodiversity hot spots.

4 THE FORESTS OF TOMORROW

This microscope image shows an open stoma, or pore, on the underside of a leaf. Stomata regulate a plant's exchange of CO_2, oxygen, water vapor, and other gases.

Human settlements, industry, and mining have reshaped the face of the earth. Overfishing has decimated the oceans. In the "Great Pacific Garbage Patch," floating human trash now covers an area twice as large as the continental United States. Emissions from human activity have changed the composition of the atmosphere. These raised levels of carbon dioxide and other gases, in turn, are influencing the climate.

As we have seen, human activities have also had a significant worldwide impact upon forests and other habitats rich in biodiversity. Some "background" level of species extinction is a normal process in the evolution of life. Species generally exist for only a few million years before dying off or evolving. Based on the evidence of the fossil record, it could be expected that, on average, one or two species might go extinct every year. During the past century, however, extinction rates have been one hundred to one thousand times higher than that. Some scientists warn that human activity could lead to another mass extinction of life on Earth.

Humans are slowly realizing that in order to preserve the planet's ecological health for future generations, we will need to better conserve natural resources. For the earth's forests, the policies and actions of world leaders could be critical in slowing deforestation and helping forests cope with other looming threats.

CLIMATE CHANGE

There is a consensus among scientists that human activity is driving climate change, but debate continues on how the effects of climate change will be manifested. For forests, it is likely that some of the first direct effects will be seen in temperature-dependent forests such as montane forests.

Montane forests are a type of tropical moist forest that grows on mountains in South America, Africa, and other areas of the world. The lowest level of growth is pre-montane forest, which gives way to lower and upper levels of montane forest. At the middle and upper levels, plant species in a subtype of forest called a cloud forest derive much of their moisture directly from the clouds in which

Ecuador's Sangay National Park, shown here, is a UN World Heritage Site. It comprises a belt of cloud forest in the Andes mountains, as well as several other biodiversity-rich hot spots.

they are shrouded and enveloped. There is a rich abundance of plant life in the canopy, such as orchids, epiphytes, and mosses that provide habitat for humming-birds, tree frogs, and other small fauna. Since they are isolated by altitude, many montane species are unique to their region. As temperatures rise, plants and animals from the premontane forest migrate upward, forcing montane species to recede. Higher temperatures can also influence cloud formation, potentially diminishing the moist cover necessary to sustain cloud forests.

Understanding how forests will respond to climate change is critical because of the forest's potential for storing carbon. If forests suffer, their role in the carbon cycle will be reduced and carbon will be released as trees decompose. If forests thrive, they could play a vital part in storing carbon and combating climate change. Scientists are using computer models and experiments to determine how climate change will affect forests. In one ongoing study, researchers at Duke University in North Carolina have been pumping tracts of outdoor forests with elevated levels of CO_2 to imitate the projected conditions fifty years in the future.

Climate change is likely to affect weather patterns. Some areas might receive less than normal precipitation, while others could see an increase. Storms and other weather events could become more severe. If temperatures rise significantly, the warming may cause moisture to evaporate from the soil more readily, drying it out. Any of these factors could disrupt forest ecosystems. Some species might thrive, some might decline, and others may migrate into different ranges.

Climate change could also worsen some of the other threats to forest health. This includes fire, insect infestations, the spread of diseases, and desertification due to environmental degradation.

In this picture, the Rouge River Hotshots battle a wildfire in Alaska's Chugach National Park in 2001. The blaze began when the U.S. Forest Service was unable to contain a controlled burn of park land.

UP IN SMOKE

Every year, there are news reports of destructive forest fires across the world, devastating swaths of Indonesia, the Amazon, and Africa. In the United States, firefighters have recently battled massive fires in California, Florida, Colorado, Idaho, Montana, and other states experiencing exceptionally dry conditions. Fires damage property and natural resources. They expose the landscape to erosion by wind and water and spew haze and pollutants into the atmosphere.

Nevertheless, fire performs a valuable and even necessary function in some ecosystems. It clears out dead vegetation and encourages regeneration. "Fire-dependent" ecosystems evolved in environments that periodically experienced fire, and life forms within these habitats developed strategies of resisting fire or recovering afterward. For example, some species of plants produce seeds that must be exposed to fire in order to germinate.

The challenge lies in managing low-intensity fires that can promote healthy forests in some ecosystems while preventing massive high-intensity fires. In the future, drought and other consequences of climate change could increase and intensify forest fires. Any strategy of managing fire must include prevention and education. According to the FAO, 80 to 90 percent of all forest fires are ignited by humans, often when fires are intentionally set to clear land but then burn out of control.

UNDER INVASION

Invasive species are non-native species that enter an ecosystem, often through human introduction. They can be animals, plants, insects, or microbes. Invasive species have no evolutionary niche in the ecosystems they enter, and they can bring about drastic and damaging changes. Native species may not be able to compete. Kudzu, for example, chokes native vegetation in some parts of the southern United States.

Native species often have no naturally evolved defense against invasive species. Insects introduced into American forests, such as the emerald ash borer and the Asian long-horned beetle, can damage and kill the trees they infest. Sometimes, invasive species can drastically

Kudzu, a vine native to Japan, has spread out of control in much of the southeastern United States, as seen here. The hardy plant can grow at a rate of a foot per day.

alter a habitat. In some forests in the United States, non-native earthworms have been introduced by fishermen who used them as bait and then dumped them near lakes. These worms eat organic matter called duff that accumulates on the forest floor. This negatively affects drainage and impacts the nutrient cycle in the forest.

Invasive species are the second greatest threat to global biodiversity next to habitat destruction. Since

Here is an Asian long-horned beetle, found on a tree at Pictured Rocks National Lakeshore in Michigan. The insect's larvae feed on the tree's wood and burrow outward, riddling the trunk with holes.

rising temperatures can allow species to migrate into new ranges, climate change could worsen the potential damage caused by invasive species as well as native scourges. Canada has recently experienced a devastating loss of pine forests due to infestations of an insect called the mountain beetle. The beetle's spread is attributed partly to warmer temperatures, since recent mild winters have not been sufficient to kill off insect populations. Forests in Colorado are also under siege by mountain pine beetles, with some foresters describing losses as catastrophic.

SUSTAINABLE DEVELOPMENT AND CONSERVATION

Deforestation statistics often seem to paint a grim picture for the future of the world's forests, but there are also encouraging signs. Many governments have made a strong commitment to maintaining healthy forests,

Corridor Ecology

Current deforestation trends around the world are leading some scientists to conclude that preserving large intact areas of forest may not be possible in the future. Instead, they believe the best way to preserve forests and other habitats is through a method called corridor ecology. Corridor ecology is a conservation strategy that consists of reconnecting isolated patches of remaining habitat—particularly forests—with other patches left over from development. Conservationists link these pieces of habitat together, sometimes by planting new growth.

In theory, the corridors will give plant and animal species room to survive in their native environment, rather than allowing them to disappear completely from a location. The strategy remains largely theoretical but is currently being tested around the world. In South America, for example, biologists are working to link patches of rain forest along Brazil's coastline. Scientists there hope that corridor ecology will help them restore part of what was once a 500,000 square mile (129,500 square kilometers) rain forest.

although poorer countries do not always have the resources to protect forests from illegal logging and other misuse. The amount of forest area designated for conservation of soil, water, and biodiversity is increasing, even in some areas with high rates of deforestation. There is a growing trend toward establishment of forest plantations and restoration of natural forest in some areas.

In order to achieve sustainable forest management practices worldwide, governments and international bodies such as the United Nations will have to address a range of related issues. Deforestation is particularly severe in countries with high rates of poverty and civil conflict. Therefore, conservation and sustainable forest management programs must include economic incentives, community involvement, and peacekeeping efforts. Forests can provide jobs in both industry and conservation. While forests can contribute to the economy through production of timber and other wood products, they can also boost lucrative recreation, tourism, and education industries. Some countries have proposed the idea of setting a monetary value to ecological services. This would range from forest user fees for recreational activities to compensation paid to governments (or other landowners) for protection of natural resources.

Poor land management tends to lead to general environmental degradation, including deforestation. In the worst cases, overgrazing or overcultivation of land can cause desertification. This loss of agricultural productivity puts further pressure on forests, as people clear even more land to compensate for infertile, desertified cropland and pasture. According to the FAO, as many as a billion people could eventually be impacted by desertification, with the highest rates occurring in sub-Saharan Africa and Latin America. Preventing and

Trees thrive on a rubber plantation in China's Yunnan province, the country's most biodiverse region, shown here. Expansion of forest plantations threatens the survival of native tropical rain forests.

reversing desertification has been a key motivator in China's expansion of forest plantations. The country has lost nearly 25 million acres (10 million hectares) of land to desertification since 1950. Drought and temperature increases due to climate change could worsen desertification in some regions.

It is estimated that the world's population will reach nine billion people by the year 2050. In order to sustain the projected population growth, it is essential that humankind develop sustainable methods of natural resource use. This is especially critical since there is now a growing demand for oil and other resources in developing countries such as India and China. The future demand for energy could have drastic consequences worldwide, with a negative impact for forests. On one hand, high energy prices are forcing some people to turn to wood for fuel. On the other, cropland in some places is being used to grow ethanol for biofuels rather than food production. Preserving forests through sustainable development will require a delicate balancing act of satisfying immediate and urgent human needs and tending to the equally vital long-term ecological health of the planet.

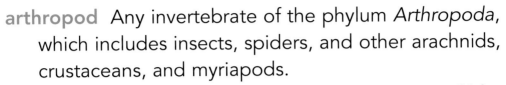

GLOSSARY

arthropod Any invertebrate of the phylum *Arthropoda*, which includes insects, spiders, and other arachnids, crustaceans, and myriapods.

biodiversity Diversity among and within species of life forms in an environment.

boreal Pertaining to the forest areas of the northern North Temperate Zone, or, more generally, pertaining to the north.

canopy The uppermost layer in the forest, formed by the leafy upper branches of the trees.

decimate To destroy completely; to ravage.

degradation A decline to a lower quality.

ecosystem A system made up of a community of organisms interacting with their environment.

epiphyte A plant that grows above the ground, supported nonparasitically by another plant or object, deriving moisture and nutrients from the air and rain.

epoch A division of geologic time.

fauna Animal life of a particular area or time period.

habitat The natural environment of an organism.

microclimate Variable conditions of a small, specific place within a larger site due to local geophysical features.

niche An organism's function or position with its ecosystem.

photosynthesis The process in which green plants use energy in sunlight to synthesize carbohydrates from carbon dioxide and water.

precipitation The falling of any form of water to the earth's surface.

rain forest A dense forest with heavy annual rainfall that recycles water back into the atmosphere from the leaves of vegetation.

subtropical Relating to a region between tropical and temperate.

transpiration The evaporation of water through pores in a plant's leaves.

FOR MORE INFORMATION

Environment Canada
70 Crémazie Street
Gatineau, PQ K1A 0H3
Canada
(819) 997-2800
Web site: http://www.ec.gc.ca/default.asp?lang=
    En&n=FD9B0E51-1
Environment Canada's mandate is to preserve and
    enhance the quality of the natural environment and
    conserve Canada's renewable and water resources.

National Resources Defense Council (NRDC)
40 West 20th Street
New York, NY 10011
(212) 727-2700
Web site: http://www.nrdc.org
NRDC is one of the nation's most effective environmental
    action groups, combining the grassroots power of
    1.2 million members and online activists with the
    courtroom clout and expertise of more than 350
    lawyers, scientists, and other professionals.

USDA Forest Service
1400 Independence Avenue SW
Washington, DC 20250-0003

(800) 832-1355

Web site: http://www.fs.fed.us

The Forest Service was established in 1905 and is an agency of the U.S. Department of Agriculture. The Forest Service manages public lands in national forests and grasslands, which encompass 193 million acres.

World Resources Institute (WRI)

10 G Street NE, Suite 800

Washington, DC 20002

(202) 729-7600

Web site: http://www.wri.org

WRI is an environmental think tank that goes beyond research to find practical ways to protect the earth and improve people's lives. Its mission is to move human society to live in ways that protect Earth's environment and its capacity to provide for the needs and aspirations of current and future generations.

WEB SITES

Due to the changing nature of Internet links, Rosen Publishing has developed an online list of Web sites related to the subject of this book. This site is updated regularly. Please use this link to access this list:

http://www.rosenlinks.com/eet/difo

FOR FURTHER READING

Chinery, Michael. *Secrets of the Rainforest: Resources and Conservation*. New York, NY: Crabtree Publishing Company, 2001.

Claybourne, Anna, et al. *The Usborne Internet-linked Encyclopedia of Planet Earth*. Tulsa, OK: Usborne Pub., 2003.

Gibson, J. Phil, and Terry R. Gibson. *Plant Diversity*. New York, NY: Chelsea House Publishers, 2007.

Kolbert, Elizabeth. *Field Notes from a Catastrophe*. New York, NY: Bloomsbury USA, 2006.

Linden, Eugene. *The Winds of Change: Climate, Weather, and the Destruction of Civilizations*. New York, NY: Simon & Schuster, 2007.

Pakenham, Thomas. *Remarkable Trees of the World*. New York, NY: W. W. Norton and Company, 2002.

Raven, Catherine. *Forestry*. New York, NY: Chelsea House Publishers, 2006.

Spray, Sharon, and Matthew D. Moran, eds. *Tropical Deforestation*. New York, NY: Roman & Littlefield Publishers, Inc., 2006.

BIBLIOGRAPHY

Barringer, Felicity. "New Battle of Logging vs. Spotted Owls Looms in West." *New York Times*, October 18, 2007. Retrieved April 2008 (http://www.nytimes.com/2007/10/18/us/18owl.html?hp).

Berger, John J. *Understanding Forests.* San Francisco, CA: Sierra Club, 1998.

Diamond, Jared. *Collapse: How Societies Choose to Fail or Succeed.* New York, NY: Viking, 2005.

Food and Agriculture Organization of the United Nations. Global Forest Resources Assessment 2005. Retrieved April 2008 (http://www.fao.org/DOCREP/008/a0400e/a0400e00.htm).

Food and Agricultural Organization of the United Nations. State of the World's Forests 2007. Retrieved April 2008 (http://www.fao.org/docrep/009/a0773e/a0773e00.htm).

Hartman, Todd. "Deaths of Trees 'Catastrophic.'" *Rocky Mountain News*, January 15, 2008. Retrieved April 2008 (http://www.rockymountainnews.com/news/2008/jan/15/beetle-infestation-get-much-worse).

Hilty, Jodi A., et al. *Corridor Ecology: The Science and Practice of Linking Landscapes for Biodiversity Conservation.* Washington, DC: Island Press, 2006.

Omi, Philip N. *Forest Fires: A Reference Handbook.* Santa Barbara, CA: ABC-CLIO, Inc., 2005.

Palmer, Douglas. *Prehistoric Past Revealed: The Four Billion Year History of Life on Earth*. Berkeley, CA: University of California Press, 2003.

Randerson, James. "Forest Experiment Questions Greenhouse Gas Strategy." *New Scientist*, April 15, 2002. Retrieved April 2008 (http://www.newscientist.com/article/dn2150-forest-experiment-questions-greenhouse-gas-strategy.html).

Reel, Monte. "Brazil Pursues Crackdown on Loggers After Surge in Cutting." *Washington Post Foreign Service*, March 21, 2008. Retrieved April 2008 (http://www.washingtonpost.com/wp-dyn/content/article/2008/03/20/AR2008032003870_pf.html).

Roberts, Jonathan. *Mythic Woods: The World's Most Remarkable Forests*. London, England: Wiedenfeld & Nicolson, 2004.

United Nations Environment Program—World Conservation Monitoring Center. "Forests." UNEP-WCMC. Retrieved April 1, 2008 (http://www.unep-wcmc.org/forest/fp_background.htm).

Warne, Kennedy. "Forests of the Tide." *National Geographic*, February 2007. Retrieved April 2008 (http://ngm.nationalgeographic.com/ngm/0702/feature5).

Williams, Michael. *Deforesting the Earth: From Prehistory to Global Crisis: An Abridgement*. Chicago, IL: University of Chicago Press, 2006.

INDEX

A

Amazon, 6, 13, 24, 38–39, 40
angiosperms, 9
arthropods, 9
Asian long-horned beetle, 49

B

biodiversity, 6, 24, 28, 31, 33–36, 38,
    42, 49, 51
biomes, 19, 22, 26

C

canopy, forest, 4, 21, 25, 34, 45
carbon cycles, 5, 18, 19–20, 39, 46
carnivores, 22
cloud forests, 45
corridor ecology, 51

D

deciduous trees, 24, 25, 33
Deforesting the Earth, 26
degradation, 6, 17, 46, 52
desertification, 46, 52–53
Devonian period, 7–8
drought, 48, 53

E

Easter Island, 14
ecosystems, 5, 8, 22, 25, 28, 40,
    46, 48
Enquiry into Plants, The, 16
environmentalists, 28, 30, 40
epiphytes, 45

F

fauna, 45
Food and Agriculture Organization
    of the United Nations (FAO),
    23, 26, 32, 41, 48, 52
forest plantations, 35, 38, 51, 53
Forest Resource Assessment (FRA), 32
forests
    and agriculture, 6, 14, 15, 16–17,
        26, 38, 52
    animal life in, 4, 9–11, 15, 18, 22,
        24, 27, 34, 38–39, 44
    boreal, 6, 19, 23, 37
    broadleaf, 24, 37
    and climate change, 11, 12–13,
        44–46, 50
    coniferous, 9, 13, 19, 24, 25, 37
    definition of, 19
    and deforestation, 6, 14, 16–17,
        26–29, 31, 33, 35–42, 44, 50–51
    and fires, 6, 9, 15, 17, 31, 32, 33,
        38, 46, 47–48
    function of, 4–5, 18, 26, 27, 39
    history of, 7–17
    and insect infestations, 32, 46,
        48–50
    logging of, 6, 17, 23, 36, 38, 40, 51
    management of, 6, 13–16, 23,
        30–31, 35–36, 50–54
    montane, 25, 44–45
    needleleaf, 24
    plant life in, 4, 7–10, 12, 15,
        21–26, 27–28, 34, 45, 48–50

rain, 5–6, 22, 24–25, 28, 33, 38, 40, 42, 51
  and reforestation, 35
  of tomorrow, 43–54

G

genetic diversity, 22–23
ginkgo trees, 9
global cooling, 11
global warming, 11, 12–13
grasslands, 9
"Great Pacific Garbage Patch," 43
greenhouse gases, 11

H

herbivores, 22

I

ice ages, 13
indigenous cultures, 28
Industrial Revolution, 20

M

mangrove swamps, 19, 25, 27
mass extinctions, 10–13, 44
mass wasting, 21

O

omnivores, 22

P

photosynthesis, 19–20
polar ice caps, 13
precipitation, 20, 21, 46

R

respiration, 19

S

secondary succession, 23
"slash and burn" methods, 25
speciation, 10
subtropical, 10, 13
sustainable development, 6, 30–31, 52–54

T

transpiration, 20

U

undergrowth, 21, 25
United Nations Environment Program, 23

W

water cycles, 18, 20–21
World Conservation Monitoring Center, 23–24

ABOUT THE AUTHOR

Corona Brezina has written more than a dozen titles for Rosen Publishing. Several of her previous books have also focused on topics related to science, social science, and current events, including *In The News: Climate Change*. She lives in Chicago.

PHOTO CREDITS

Cover, pp. 1, 11, 29 © Getty Images; pp. 4–5, 7, 34, 49 © National Geographic/Getty Images; p. 8 © Chase Studio/Photo Researchers; pp. 12, 30 © AFP/Getty Images; p. 16 © Smithsonian American Art Museum, Washington, D.C./Art Resource, NY; pp. 18, 39 © Aurora/Getty Images; p. 22 © Sally Bensusen/Photo Researchers; p. 25 © Kevin Schafer/Alamy; p. 32 © Tim Graham/Getty Images; pp. 40, 47 © AP Photos; p. 43 © Susumu Nishinaga/Photo Researchers; p. 45 © Kevin Schafer/Peter Arnold; p. 50 © Edward Kinsman/Photo Researchers; p. 53 © Zhu Hua.

Designer: Tom Forget; Photo Researcher: Marty Levick